CU00641374

Dorchester

IN OLD PHOTOGRAPHS

Aerial view of Dorchester, the county town of Dorset.

Dorchester

IN OLD PHOTOGRAPHS

TED GOSLING

Alan Sutton Publishing Limited
Phoenix Mill · Far Thrupp · Stroud
Gloucestershire · GL5 2BU

First published 1994

Copyright © Ted Gosling, 1994

Cover photograph: Hangman's Cottage *c*. 1910.

British Library Cataloguing in Publication Data.
A catalogue record for this book is available from
the British Library.

ISBN 0-7509-0748-7

Typeset in 9/10 Sabon.
Typesetting and origination by
Alan Sutton Publishing Limited.
Printed in Great Britain by
Ebenezer Baylis, Worcester.

Contents

The arch at the entrance to High East Street was put up by the Borough Council for the Bath and West Show in 1908.

Foreword

Having spent a lifetime in magazine and newspaper publishing and, in retirement, having served as a trustee and steward in a local museum, I have long been aware of the considerable and widespread interest in the past. It takes many forms, from a fascination with fossils of creatures which lived hundreds of thousands, if not millions, of years ago, right down to events and places and things within living memory.

Today's youngsters find it almost impossible to imagine life when I was at their age. In those days there were certainly more horses than motor cars in our streets. All the tradesmen weighed goods with brass or iron weights on scales. Luggage and parcels came from the railway station on a dray – a sort of platform on four large iron-bound wooden wheels, drawn by two superb Shire horses.

If you wanted, and could afford it, a radio was constructed for you, probably by a radio mechanic from the First World War. On Sunday evening our parlour was always full to overflowing with neighbours who came to hear the church service from St Martins in the Fields – 150 miles away! A minor miracle.

Walter John Burden, boot maker, 8 Church Street, *c.* 1935. At the time this picture was taken, Burden's had traded for over one hundred years.

The Dorchester Brewery, *c.* 1895. The brewery belonged to Eldridge Pope and Co. and was built in 1880. The firm had a history that extended back over many years and at the time this photograph was taken it was successfully trading throughout the south of England. The brewery's speciality was a palatable drink known as Crystal Ale – this could be shipped in bottles to all parts of the tropics and arrive in perfect condition.

Photography in the last 160 years has recorded the past superbly, going back far beyond memory, although sometimes it is a past that seems almost touchable. It is very important that collections of those photographs have been built up and are now published for our interest.

The author of this book has an excellent collection covering, especially, Seaton in Devon and the villages and country around. He has cooperated with the Dorchester Museum in producing this volume, using over two hundred photographs from their archives. Dorchester deserves to be recorded, for not only is it an excellent county town, it also has a continuous recorded history going back, with ample evidence, about six thousand years to early neolithic times.

At a little distance, and well recorded elsewhere, is Maiden Castle, a huge Iron Age hill-fort, which has within it a neolithic causewayed camp and a huge bank barrow of the same period, one of only ten in Britain.

Within the town area is the henge at Maumbury, converted to an amphitheatre by the Romans and used until recent times for festivals and celebrations. Poundbury, also of pre-historic origin, was used in the First World War as a prisoner of war camp, and throughout the city there are many buildings of historic interest. This book records them, the people and their costume, transport, special events and so much more.

We have to be grateful to the author, the Dorchester Museum and the photographers, whoever they were, for this excellent record – not only for our enjoyment and interest, but for the folk in the future, who will see us as a part of their past.

Norman Whinfrey

SECTION ONE

The Early Days

Bowling Alley Walk, looking eastward towards Trinity Street, 1858.

One of the earliest photographs of the town, showing the Kings Arms Hotel, High East Street, *c.* 1850. At the time the hotel was the principal coaching inn and Royal Mail staging post. It had stabling for 120 horses and was well known and popular with the county people.

A strange, atmospheric photograph of Dorchester Cemetery, *c.* 1859.

The west side of Cornhill, *c.* 1855. Careful examination reveals that the quite natural looking group of individuals outside the Antelope Hotel has been skilfully posed – a time exposure of thirty seconds would have been required. At the time this photograph was taken, a dispensing chemist called Durden had a shop next to the Antelope.

South Street and Cornhill Eastside, 1859. Note the condition of the road – on a wet day it must have been impossible to cross without getting your feet muddy. The obelisk in the centre of the road at the top is the old town pump, and the shop on the top right-hand corner was Jacob's hat shop.

Looking up South Street, 1868. Napper's Mite, with its clock supported by a Gothic bracket, is on the right and next door is the Grammar School. In 1879 the school was replaced by a three-storey block, which still stands today. South Street is now pedestrianized for most of its length, something which was obviously not necessary at this time, when neighbours could stop and chat with no fear of being knocked down.

Holy Trinity Church, photographed before 1875 when it was rebuilt in its present form at a cost of £6,000. This church replaced a previous one which had been destroyed by fire in 1824.

Dorset County Hospital, *c.* 1859. The hospital was opened in 1841 in what is now the north wing. The main block was built in 1845 and the south wing added in 1859. It was built and supported by voluntary contributions from Dorset people, the Williamses of Bridehead prominent among them. The architect was Benjamin Ferrey, and although it was built in stages the design was consistent – a pleasant simple version of an Elizabethan Dorset manorhouse. Ferrey may have been assisted in this, and other works in Dorchester, by Arthur D.H. Acland, who changed his name to Troyte as a condition of a bequest in 1852. He practised as an amateur architect; one of his works is the monument to Admiral Hardy at Portesham.

The west side of South Street, 1859. Note the unmade road. The man standing in his doorway is wearing the stove-pipe hat of the period. The sign-board outside the shop on the left advertises newspapers from the Society for Promoting Christian Knowledge.

High West Street, *c.* 1870. Modern motor traffic may have brought many advantages to our communities, but at what cost? This delightful photograph evokes a sense of peace and quiet that is no longer apparent in our towns.

Bishops Nurseries, 1875.

Beggar's Knap, Dorchester, *c.* 1875. This is the junction of Great Western Road with Weymouth Avenue – note the Junction Hotel on the corner.

Presentation to Mrs Bingham, wife of Col. Bingham, the commander of the Dorset Militia, at the barracks, June 1866. The unknown photographer captured many of the fashions which were popular nearly 130 years ago: ladies wearing those incredibly long, stuffy dresses, and soldiers in baggy trousers and bulging frock-coats.

Looking up Weymouth Avenue, *c.* 1875. A hay wagon coming down the lane would have been a common sight in a rural community that had hardly changed for generations. The author Thomas Hardy would have been familiar with scenes like this, his books of peasant life and the countryside of Dorset being based on such agricultural communities.

The north side of High West Street, *c.* 1858.

Assize Court, High West Street, *c*. 1860. The scene has hardly altered today. The Shire Hall was built in 1796–7 to the design of Thomas Hardwick of London and is elegantly utilitarian. Dorchester had been the usual, though not the invariable, venue of the Judgeson Assize in Dorset since the Middle Ages, and the Crown Court, little altered since it was opened, was used continuously for the Assizes until the opening of the present court in the new County Hall. It was here, in 1834, that the Tolpuddle martyrs were sentenced to transportation to Botany Bay for having taken oaths binding them to membership of a trade union. Their sentences were repealed two years later in response to public feeling, and they were able to return to England in 1838. There was originally another court, the Nisi Prius Court, which was adapted for use by the newly formed County Council in 1889. Since the fourteenth century county affairs had been conducted by the Justices of the Peace at Quarter Sessions, which were held in various Dorset towns until the beginning of the nineteenth century, after which they were usually held at the Shire Hall in Dorchester. Their administrative powers were largely transferred to the elected County Council, set up under the Local Government Act of 1888. Since then the scope of the County Council's powers has been much extended, and the county administration is now centred on County Hall.

South Walk, west end, from Bowling Alley Walk, *c.* 1860.

Engine No. 8, *Vesta*, Dorchester, *c.* 1858. This was a South Western engine built by Sharp Roberts in 1838, of their standard design. Two horizontal cylinders worked a double cranked axle in the driving wheels. The engine driver and his fireman were exposed to all wind and weathers; it must have been a cold, wet job on long journeys in the winter.

SECTION TWO

The Town

Cornhill, on the left, and High West Street, on the right, *c.* 1890. The town pump can just be seen on the extreme left. Howes refreshment rooms on the corner provided soup, chops, steaks, teas, coffee and bottled ales. Morton's Boot Stores next to the Antelope were noted for service and quality.

High West Street, 1930. The tobacconist shop on the corner of Cornhill and High East Street belonged to Edward Albert Riglar. The half-timbered building on the right (just behind the parked car) is known as Judge Jeffreys' Lodgings, and dates from the early seventeenth century. Judge Jeffreys was thought to have lodged here during or after the Monmouth Rebellion of 1685. The motor bike in the foreground is a 1929 Ariel and carries the Dorset registration number of TK.

South Court, South Walk Road, *c.* 1899. At this time South Court was the home of Alfred Pope who, with his brother Edwin, had acquired full control of the Edridge Pope Brewery. A friend of Thomas Hardy, Alfred helped found the firm that now owns pubs throughout the country.

St Peter's Church, *c.* 1960. This photograph was taken in the few days between the demolition and erection of buildings in North Square (formerly the Bull Stoke). All ancient prints, plans and maps indicate that at no other time in the last four hundred years would it have been possible, from this spot, to record the beauty of this fine example of Perpendicular work. The church has many features in common with Sherborne Abbey, reputed to be the work of the same architect. It was built about 1450 on the site of former churches which had originated with the Roman town of Durnovaria. It was one of six buildings to escape the fire of 1613, and is the oldest building in the town. In the seventeenth century the Revd John White, a puritan divine and one of the founders of Massachusetts, ministered in this church.

Dorchester artillery barracks, *c.* 1900.

High East Street with the Phoenix Hotel on the left, *c.* 1896. The Phoenix provided good family and commercial accommodation and was noted for its excellent fare. The spire belongs to All Saints' Church.

High West Street, *c.* 1895. The Shire Hall is on the left, with the embattled 90 ft tower of St Peter's in the background.

Looking down the tree-lined West Walk, *c.* 1895.

Colliton Walk, 1898.

South Street, 1895.

Two old houses in High West Street, *c.* 1890. The house with the balustraded galleries (to the left of the two people by the kerb) is Judge Jeffreys' Lodgings.

Howe's Corner, *c*. 1888. This building was demolished in 1903.

St Peter's Church after a heavy fall of snow, *c*. 1892. Howe's confectioner's shop stands on the corner of Cornhill.

High East Street, *c.* 1885. The droppings on the road are proof that the horse ruled supreme.

High East Street, *c.* 1880. Apart from the unmade road, dusty in summer and muddy in winter, and the names above the shops, the appearance of the street is not vastly different today. In those days all the shops were privately owned, and the owner usually lived behind and over his shop. Every morning he would make sure that the pavements in front were washed, and great deference was shown to the carriage trade.

Boots, c. 1960. Before Boots took over this site, Ernest Bailey had a ladies' drapers shop here. Boots enlarged the premises to its present size in 1974.

The site of the present Marks & Spencer store in South Street, 9 April 1936. The building contractors were Bovis and the architect A.E. Batzer. The Plaza in Trinity Street can be seen in the background. The cinema cost approximately £20,000 to build and opened in 1933; at this time 'going to the pictures' was a favourite family entertainment.

Borough Gardens, 1922.

A delightful and superbly balanced period photograph of a couple posing outside Hangman's Cottage, *c.* 1910.

This fine bronze statue of William Barnes (1801–86), the dialect poet of Dorset, is by Roscoe Mullins and stands at the foot of the tower of St Peter's Church in High West Street. William Barnes, much loved in his native county, had a great knowledge and understanding of Dorset and is best remembered for his dialect verse. Many consider his best work to be 'The Geate a-vallen to ', which he wrote near the close of his life.

The Cenotaph and South Walk, 1922. The Cenotaph, which is in the centre of the town, was unveiled by Col. the Rt. Hon. Lord Ellenborough CB on Empire Day 1921. It was designed and executed by Messrs Grassby and Son, under the supervision of the then Maj. A.L.T. Tilley Esq. It is 14 ft high, and over 20 tons of Portland stone was used in its construction. The names of 230 men are inscribed, reminding future generations of how much was given to secure a peaceful world.

The Junction Hotel, 1909.

South Walk from South Street, *c.* 1900.

Looking up the tree-lined Bridport Road, *c.* 1880. The boys on the left, relaxing in the afternoon sun, and the deserted country lane present a delightful picture.

Napper's Mite and the Grammar School, 1903. Napper's Mite was built in 1615 by Sir Robert Napper as an almshouse for ten people. In 1843 the façade was largely rebuilt in the manner shown, with a clock supported on a Gothic bracket. The almshouses have now been converted into an attractive shopping precinct, with Napper's Mite Coffee Lounge facing South Street. The Grammar School was founded by Thomas Hardye of Frampton in 1569 and occupied an old stone building next to Napper's Mite. This was replaced in 1879 by the three-storey block seen here. Note the poster advertising the Royal Counties Show at Southampton.

Looking down Cornhill, 1930.

Aerial view of Dorchester, *c.* 1938.

High West Street, 1895.

High East Street, 1890. Taken by Francis Frith, this photograph is reminiscent of the work of Paul Martin, the famous and very gifted Victorian photographer noted for his street pictures of working-class life in London.

Weymouth Road, *c.* 1892. This appears to be a photograph of the road widening near the Junction Hotel.

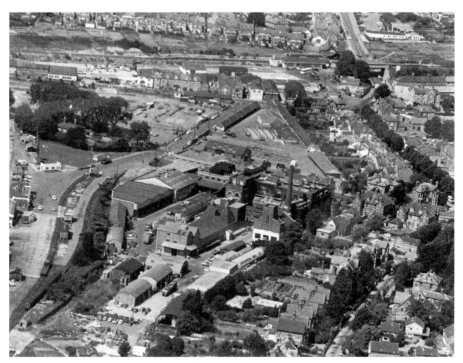

Aerial view of Dorchester, *c.* 1938. You can see the brewery and tall chimney of Messrs Eldridge Pope & Co. Ltd, with its commanding position in Weymouth Avenue, adjoining the Southern Railway station. The brewery buildings were erected in 1879–80.

Lewers Carriage Works, at the junction of South Street and Weymouth Avenue, c. 1860. Judging by the onlookers, photography was still unusual enough to attract attention.

Looking up South Street, c. 1894. Virgin's shop is now the site of the post office.

Borough Gardens, 1898. The Borough Gardens in Cornwall Road were purchased and laid out by the Corporation in 1896. The bandstand was erected in 1898.

Dorchester viewed across the fields, 1891.

South Street, *c.* 1890. A baker and confectioner's shop named George occupied 2 South Street: it also had Dining Rooms for morning coffee and luncheons. The premises on the left was a ladies' and gents' haircutting salon, and the house just visible on the right belonged to W. Burt, surgeon and dentist.

Thomas Pouncy's tobacconist shop, 3 Cornhill, 1920. Thomas Pouncy was also a saddler and a collector of taxes for Dorchester St Peter's.

A charming photograph of High West Street, *c.* 1891. The little girl is wearing clothes typical of the period – woollen stockings and boots, and a frilly white apron to keep her dress clean. Note the distinctively shaped push-chair on the pavement.

High West Street after a heavy fall of snow, 1881.

Looking up High East Street, c. 1899. Although the main road into the town was then metalled, it was thick with dust in the summer and muddy in the winter.

High West Street with St Peter's Church, c. 1890.

Dorchester prison, 1965. The prison stands on a spur, with a short steep slope down to the River Frome. This is the site of the medieval Dorchester Castle, of which little is known. According to the newly accepted principles of John Howard, the penal reformer, a county prison was built on the site in 1783. The present buildings, however, date largely from the 1880s, soon after central government had taken over control of the prison and other county gaols, previously governed by the County Quarter Sessions.

Back of South Street, c. 1901. The premises are probably those of Timms and John Pouncy.

High West Street and the corner of Trinity Street, *c.* 1920. Genge draper's shop is on the corner, and the building on the extreme left was once a soda-water factory, which survived until Genge's was rebuilt in the late 1920s.

Jackmans of 28 and 29 High East Street, before the First World War. Jackmans were tailors, clothiers, outfitters, hosiers and boot and shoe factors. It appears that the shop has just taken delivery of new stock, judging by the large baskets on the pavement.

High East Street with All Saints' Church on the left, *c.* 1901. The church was rebuilt in 1845 in the Early English style. It was designed by Benjamin Ferrey, the architect who was responsible for the Town Hall and the Dorset County Hospital. The north-west tower, with the spire, is a notable landmark in the town.

A picturesque view of the River Frome, 1913.

Hangman's Cottage, 1898. The cottage was so named because of the local belief that the public executioner lived here during the time of the Bloody Assize in 1685, when Judge Jeffreys tried the unhappy people who were implicated in the Monmouth Rebellion.

Borough Gardens, just after they were opened in 1896. The bandstand was erected two years later.

The amphitheatre, Maumbury Rings, 1891. The building in the background is the South Western station. The Roman amphitheatre, an oval of 218 ft by 163 ft inside, was used in the seventeenth and eighteenth centuries as a place of execution. In 1705 crowds of people came to witness the death of Mary Channing, who was strangled and then burned for poisoning her husband.

The town pump, Cornhill, *c.* 1874. The pump was erected in 1784, on the site of an old market building. St Peter's Church and the Corn Exchange are in the background.

Cornhill, *c.* 1900. Note Boons Stores and the post office on the left-hand side.

Bridport Road, looking east, near Top o' Town, *c.* 1900. The notice in the road belonged to the Borough of Dorchester, and says that this road was 'stopped' during repairs. They were obviously tree-felling, and this had attracted a group of interested spectators.

The Grove, 1887.

The Crown Inn (now demolished) on Durngate Street, *c.* 1900.

High East Street, *c.* 1890. The shop on the left was occupied by Henry Line, the stationer and bookseller.

Top o' Town, High West Street, 1922. The lady cyclist is able to push her bicycle across the road in comparative safety.

High Street West and Trinity Church, 1922. The Model T Ford parked on the right carries the Dorset registration number FX 8792.

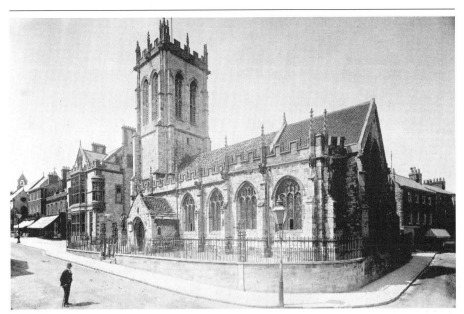

St Peter's Church, *c.* 1895. The County Museum is to the left of the church and to the extreme left of the photograph the church of the Holy Trinity is just visible. This photograph was taken by William Willis (1841–1923), using the photographic process called Platinotype, which he had invented. As the name suggests, the process involved platinum, which was used instead of silver salts for coating the print and gave the finished photograph a soft, silver-grey appearance.

The rear of 4 Princes Street, photographed on 19 August 1958 just before it was demolished.

The Kings Arms, *c.* 1920. During the mid-nineteenth century more than forty coaches a week changed horses at the Kings Arms, and during its long history many people have visited the hotel. Queen Victoria stayed here in 1853 after reviewing the fleet, and Edward VII, when Prince of Wales, stayed here while on walking and shooting expeditions. Thomas Hardy lunched regularly at the hotel, and other famous visitors have included Lawrence of Arabia, who put up friends here when he was visiting Clouds Hill, the Dorset poet William Barnes, Augustus John, Pavlova, and the three Powys brothers. In recent years both Prince Charles and Prince Andrew have lunched in the hotel during active service at Portland.

Just People

Dorchester Young Men's Christian Association, 1899. The photographer has succeeded in persuading everyone in this large group to look at the camera.

The caption on the back of this photograph gives the information that this is the 'Tom Warne Presentation', but the date and occasion are unknown.

Gideon Wright and his staff, of Wright & Son, Higher East Street, *c.* 1900. Gideon Wright is seated centre, and members of his staff include Joe and Harry Beck, Jimmy Steads, Jack Lock, Charles Amey and Robert Wright.

St Peter's Sunday School outing, *c*. 1926. Those present include Mr and Mrs Norris, Mrs Markby, Miss Lewis, Miss Frisby, Archie Markby, Daisy Coates.

St Peter's Sunday School outing to Osmington, *c*. 1927. The group includes Revd A. Markby and Mrs Markby, Miss Kathleen Escott, Miss Merrick, Miss Lewis and Miss Frisby.

Members of the choir at the church of St Mary the Virgin. The church was built as late as 1911, but in a fourteenth-century style.

The staff of Dorchester Steam Laundry at the firm's Christmas party, 1922.

Staff of Maud Road School, 1951. Back row, left to right: Mrs Lewis, -?-, Mrs Stansfield, Mrs Pinkney, Mrs Bellamy, Mr Rawlings. Second row: Miss Pafford, Miss Bishop, Miss Rooke, Mrs Toop, Mrs Woodward, Miss Downing, Miss Cookman, Miss Milne. Front row: Mrs Delhaise, Miss Lewis, Miss Edwards, Miss Williams (headmistress), Miss Foot, Miss Good, Mrs Woodward.

Staff of Maud Road School, 1953. Back row, left to right: Mr Rawlings, Mrs Hayer, Mrs Bellamy, Mrs Stansfield, -?-, Mrs Lewis. Second row: Miss Norton, Miss Pafford, Miss Good, Miss Lewis, Mrs Woodward, -?-, Miss Rooke, Mrs Woodward, Miss Foot, Mrs Pinkney. Front row: Miss Bishop, Miss Milne, Miss Williams (headmistress), Mrs Delhaise, Mrs Toop, Mrs Tidball.

A group of dignified gentlemen, possibly Borough officials, 2 July 1901. Although taken on the same date as the photograph opposite, no other details of the occasion or subject of this photograph are known. Any additional information would be welcome.

Dorchester Unemployment Centre, 1930. The slump of 1929, with cuts in wages, resulted in a rising tide of unemployment which caused much unrest throughout the country. Men who a few years before had fought for King and Country were now spending the day looking for work. Here we see some of the men in Dorchester who, apart from living in poverty, had to experience the personal indignity of the means test.

Beating the Bounds, Borough of Dorchester, 2 July 1901. Back row, left to right: F.J. Holland, W.E. Groves, T.A. Pearce, G.J. Hunt, E.W. Wescott, S. Sansford, Dr W.B. Cosens, J. Feacey, S.D. Allen, H. Stedman, S.H. Stroud. Second row: G. Mitchell, A.H. Edwards, Dr E.J. Day, A.L.T. Tilley, J. Pain, T.H. Tilley, W.J. Bellinger, J. Vincent, S. Clist. Third row: J. Porter, G.J. Dennis, T.R. Higgins, A.G. Symonds, G. Davis (Mayor), J.W. Fudge, J. Hazel, Dr E.W. Kerr. Front row: T. Higgins, A. Trim, A. Allen, W. Young, K. Fudge, H. Tilley. The ceremony was an annual event, dating back to the times when literacy was uncommon. The burgesses and villagers of a borough or parish traversed the boundaries of their areas. They would beat the boundary with sticks as an aid to memory, as written directions were useless.

Dorchester Commercial School Scout troop in the school grounds, 22 Trinity Street, 1909. Mr A.V. Dodderidge, the school principal who founded the troop, is on the left, with Mr L.J. Medway, the scoutmaster, on the right. The Scouts include Smither, Gillingham, Parsons, Duffett, Miller, Christopher, Sherry, Parham, Parsons, Griffin, Selway and Bugler.

C.A. Barrett (third from left) in his workshop, 1902. Barrett & Sons were builders, painters and decorators with premises in South Street. C.A. Barrett died in 1904. The small boy sitting on the bench is Master Percival Cyril Peter Barrett, who died in 1981, aged 82.

Dorchester Fire Brigade, 1926. Their engine, *Leonie*, was named after Mrs Hodges, wife of the Fire Brigade Committee chairman. Standing proudly on the left is the brigade captain, Mr Jewell. The other firemen include Messrs Membury, Lock, Payne, Elsley, Pope, Payner, Rogers, Bowering, Baker, Rawlins and, standing to the right, A.R. Jeffery, the brigade lieutenant.

Dorchester Grammar School, *c.* 1894. The Grammar School was founded in 1569 by Thomas Hardye of Frampton. The headmaster, Mr Kingdon, is in the centre, with members of staff including Messrs Cooper, House and Lenton. Pupils include Saunders, Wright, Hodges, Land, Lock, Greening, Hawkins, Linton, Tilley, Edwards and Goldie.

Women's Institute Fair in the Corn Exchange, 1922.

An old labourer in Dorchester Workhouse, *c.* 1890. Nothing is known about the identity of this man, but it is clear from his bearing that he was not too happy to pose for the camera. We are left with an image caught on film from a time when the elderly lacked the security of the Welfare State and lived in fear of the workhouse.

West Mills Ironworks, Millers Close, *c.* 1932. Mr J. Gifford senior is standing in the background by the window in the centre of the photograph, while Mr J. Gifford junior is in front of the right-hand window. Mr Jack Way is working the saw bench on the left, and Mr H.C. Gifford the one in the centre.

The staff of Boons Stores Ltd of South Street, before 1906. Wearing a boater with a decorative band (back row, centre) is Oliver Boon, the proprietor. Directly on his left, wearing a stetson-type hat, is his brother, Fred, who went to live in New Brunswick, Canada, in 1906.

Barrett & Sons, builders, Dorchester, *c*. 1895. The staff were noted tradesmen, and took a tremendous pride in their job.

Ralph Channon with the aeroplane he constructed, 1909. Channon began construction in May 1909, and the aeroplane was taken to Maiden Castle for its first flight on 20 November 1909. The original idea had been that she would slide down the steep hill to take off, but she would not move. Wheels were therefore placed beneath the craft that would drop off as she left the ground. Ralph's brother, E.H. Channon, helped with the construction, and went for a short flight in July 1910. The plane had a White and Poppe six-cylinder engine, but the screw and gearing were all made by the Channons.

Dorchester Borough fire station, *c.* 1895, with fire brigade members and officials on parade.

A Methodist Church wedding group, 1909. Although this photograph was posed, it is still a good record of social history, showing the clothes worn for this sort of occasion at that time. The visual and social significance of the hat was still important when this party faced the photographer.

The staff of Genge Dixon and Jameson, 1899. This well-arranged group photograph, with Mr and Mrs Dixon seated in the middle, is typical of the period.

Mr Pass, the Earl of Shaftesbury, Mr Gale and Canon Morrow opening Maiden Castle House, 1948.

The staff of Thurman's, with their wives and children, at Thurman's Flower Show, August 1938. This event also coincided with Mr H. King's fiftieth anniversary with the firm.

A group of local musicians around the turn of the century. Members include Alice Ridley, Lucy Ridley, Florence Ridley and Captain Acland.

Dorchester Women's Institute event. No date or details of this photograph are known; any information would be appreciated.

SECTION FOUR

Events

Councillor Frederick Chas James, wearing the white countryman's smock, and, next to him, Miss Winifride Marsden, the Mayor of Dorchester, 1936. Among others in the photograph are Mrs James, the Mayoress, Councillor Lawrence Charles Lyndon Moore and Mr I. Skyrme. Everyone appears to be enjoying themselves, although the event is unknown.

The Cattistock Hunt meet in Dorchester, *c.* 1900. This hunt had kennels at Cattistock, and the pack comprised sixty couples of foxhounds. In those days they hunted on Monday, Tuesday, Wednesday, Friday and Saturday.

Procession in High West Street, *c.* 1900. The men in front carry an international banner, but no details are known of the event, or the exact date.

Dray horses belonging to the brewers Strong's of Romsey, going up Maumbury Road at the turn of the century – a reminder of how much depended in those days on the muscle power of horse and man. The draymen include Fred Tucker, Bill Amey, Messrs Nothern, Hawker and Adams. The caption on the photograph reads '4 mph all day'.

Dorchester Fire Brigade at Winterborne Came House, *c*. 1903. Judging by their smart appearance, the brigade were not answering a 'shout', but had gone to Came House for some special occasion. Came House, a large mansion of Portland stone, was built in 1756 by the Damer family and stood in a park of over 230 acres. It was to Winterborne Came Rectory that William Barnes, the Dorset dialect poet, came to live in 1862.

Queen Victoria's diamond jubilee celebrations, held in the Roman amphitheatre, Maumbury Rings, Dorchester, 1897. A service was held as part of the proceedings. The possibility of a great celebration was first discussed after the jubilee of 1887, although it was not until 1896 that public interest was thoroughly aroused. Every town and village formed a committee for the great day, and streets everywhere were lavishly decorated.

A confirmation service at St Peter's, conducted by the Bishop of Salisbury, *c.* 1910.

The people of Dorchester listen to the Mayor read the letter from the Privy Council and the proclamation of George V in May 1910, following the death of George's father, Edward VII, on 6 May.

The Prince of Wales, later King Edward VIII and the Duke of Windsor, greets officials at Top o' Town during his visit to Dorchester, 20 July 1923. He is flanked by his entourage and the Mayor, Lorenzo Ernest Ling.

The Prince devoted much time and energy to the needs of ex-servicemen. During his visit he met some of the local soldiers and sailors who had fought during the First World War.

The provincial tours that the Prince of Wales made during the 1920s were a conspicuous feature of his public life, and local dignitaries greeted him with pompous formalities which at times he must have found a strain.

Loved for his charm, his humility and his goodwill, the Prince received an ecstatic reception wherever he went. Everybody wanted to get close to him and to touch him; by the end of these visits he was often covered with bruises.

The arrival of the Princess Royal at Dorchester for her visit on 1 May 1930. She was greeted by the Mayor and other local dignitaries.

Civic luncheon in connection with the visit of the Lord Mayor and Sheriffs of London to Dorchester on 18 July 1936. At the centre of the top table is E.C. James, Mayor of Dorchester, with the Lord Mayor and Mrs James, then one of the Sheriffs of London, on his right. On Mr James's left is the Sheriff of Dorset, then the other Sheriff of London. Other guests include Aldermen Wheeler, Pope, Walne, Tilley, Hunt and Underwood, Revd Williams, Councillors Pope, Stroud, Harding, Beavis, Fare, Rossiter, Jewell, Moore and Jeffery, Lord Staverdale, Mr Edwards, Mr Strange, Mr Ferris, Mr Biles, Mr Chick and Mr Duforse (President of NFU).

Lt.-Com. Hector Monro, High Sheriff of Dorset, leading the judge and court officials to the Assizes, *c.* 1931.

Canon Hiver and the Revd Bowden Smith on the top of St Peter's Church tower on St Peter's Day, *c.* 1925.

The visit of Edward, Prince of Wales, 1887. The Prince, arriving from Weymouth, is turning into Great Western Avenue. Unlike his mother, Queen Victoria, the Prince of Wales liked all men to know where he was and what he was up to. He welcomed publicity, and in return the people loved him. Every street was gay with bunting, and the town presented a most animated and picturesque scene.

High West Street decorated for the coronation of King Edward VII, 1902. The event had had to be postponed due to a surgical operation, and the whole country had prayed for the King's recovery. The postponed celebration took place six weeks later, and the day was observed as a general holiday.

The service held at Maumbury Rings on the coronation of King Edward VII, 9 August 1902. Few men in our history have fitted the role of kingship more exactly than King Edward VII; he gloried in the sceptre. His reign was regarded as an Edwardian summer, when the sunshine was truly golden.

Carnival tableau, c. 1936. The colourful spectacle of the carnival was as much a part of the Dorchester calendar as the seasons of sowing, harvest and Christmas. Before the Second World War, thousands of people lined the route on such occasions and cheered on floats like this.

Icen Way School float in the 1937 carnival.

Matron Bingerfield, Sister Purchase and Sister Griffiths, with other staff, study the model of the projected new Nurses' Home for Dorset County Hospital, *c.* 1936.

Opening The Gables as a children's home, 17 June 1950.

Poundbury Fair, *c.* 1902. This large fair, held at Poundbury on the last Thursday in September, was an important event in the calendar of the local farming community. Farming was then, as now, a busy way of life, and fair days like this provided a rare opportunity to relax, meet people, exchange news and hear other farmers talk about the hard times they were having.

Dorchester agricultural engineers Lott & Walne display the latest in farm implements at the 1887 Bath and West Show.

Poundbury Sheep Fair, *c.* 1920.

A large crowd gathered to watch Sir George Williams, a local dignitary, lay the foundation stone of the YMCA building, 1898.

The Dorchester Vocal Association at a concert given in the Corn Exchange, 1898. The conductor is Mr Boyton Smith and the charming lady violinist second from the left in the front row is Mrs Dodderidge.

Spare Time exhibition at the Corn Exchange, 1896. The exhibits shown were all of a high standard. The dolls on the table at the front were made by children in the 'under 14' class.

Borough Gardens, 1910. The officials on the bandstand and the large crowd indicate some kind of event, but no details are known. Any information on the occasion would be welcome.

Dance of the Plough, performed by the Iwerne Minster Folk Dancers, 1939. Thomas Hardy, in his account of the Christmas mummers on Egdon Heath in *The Return of the Native*, remarks that the genuine survival of a tradition can be distinguished from the modern revival of a tradition because in the latter the performers will appear enthusiastic whereas in the former they will seem to be carrying out their task with a sense of dreary obligation. The Iwerne Minster Folk Dancers appear to qualify for the modern revival.

Visit of the Prince of Wales, later King Edward VII, to Dorchester and the Bath and West Show, 1887. The Prince of Wales was popular, and High East Street was richly decorated for the occasion.

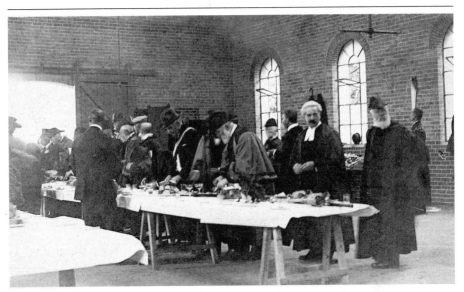

The Butter Street buffet at 1 p.m. on the coronation day of King George V, 1911.

The Procession in Maumbury Rings.

Rain fell during the afternoon of the coronation day, which put a wet blanket on the procession at Maumbury Rings.

The proclamation of King Edward VII, Dorchester, 26 January 1901. Queen Victoria died on 22 January 1901, and the successor to the throne was her son, the Prince of Wales. Here the people of Dorchester listen to the Mayor read the letter from the Privy Council and the proclamation. The soldiers stood to attention, and for the first time in sixty years the crowd sang 'God Save the King'.

Procession emerging from South Street and passing Tilley & Son Motor Showroom, c. 1910. The exact date and occasion is unknown, and any information would be welcome.

Dorchester Michaelmas market, 1907.

An ox roast is prepared as part of the celebrations on the coronation of George V, Dorchester, 22 June 1911. The ox had been donated by James Foot. The coronation of George V was a day for celebrations throughout the country. Every town and village formed a committee to arrange activities for the great day, and everywhere the streets were lavishly decorated. Processions, parties, sports and many other attractions were the order of the day, and the memory of these celebrations stayed with people for the rest of their lives.

Passive resisters to the new education rate introduced in 1902. They objected to any religion, even their own, being taught in schools, and refused to pay the rate. They were charged at Dorchester Magistrates Court and, after the hearing, posed outside the Corn Exchange.

The Dorchester British Legion Band in concert, 4 August 1923. Their uniforms were supplied by Jackman's.

Colliton Street (C of E) Boys' School pupils, *c.* 1912. The school was established in 1812 and enlarged in 1908 to provide for 532 boys. The pupils, shod in hob-nailed boots so typical of this period, are proudly displaying their medals and the sports shield.

The Military

The Dorset Volunteers at camp, *c.* 1875. The Volunteers would arrive in the town for training, led by the fifes and drums. Training was done in the summer between the hay and corn harvests, and each day began at 5.00 a.m. with a bugle call to muster, followed by two hours of drill.

This photograph is captioned 'The Barrack Square, Poundbury, *c.* 1880', and the men are standing outside the officer's house. The traditions and achievements of the Victorian army were splendid, and these officers were part of a force that helped to build the British Empire.

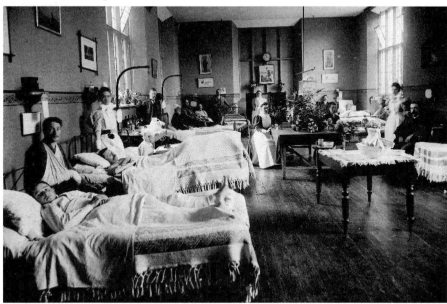

The men's ward, Dorset County Hospital, Princes Street, 1886. The hospital was established in 1841, and a wing added in 1859.

Barrack Gate, the entrance to the Dorsetshire Regiment infantry barracks, 1890. Built in 1879, this gatehouse is now The Keep military museum.

The Triumphal Arch, South Street, *c.* 1901. Because the Boer War in South Africa was such a lengthy conflict, waiting companies of Volunteers had to be called up. In 1901 Dorchester welcomed back the first of those men, the gallant Rifle Volunteers. They arrived amid tumultuous cheering and the ringing of church bells. The arch was erected to mark their home-coming.

The arch at the entrance to South Street, decorated at the end of the Boer War, 1902. The war had clouded the last years of Queen Victoria's reign and there were wild rejoicings throughout the country when hostilities ceased. In Dorchester the return of the Dorsets was greeted with widespread enthusiasm. The town was gaily decorated with flags and streamers, with triumphal arches spanning the roadway at various points, and the troops returned to the town to the accompaniment of cheers from the jubilant crowds.

The Band of the 4th Battalion Dorsets, 1912. Dorchester was the depot of Regimental District No. 39, The Dorsetshire Regiment.

The Scots Greys passing down High West Street before the First World War.

4th Battalion, Dorset Regiment saw service in India and Mesopotamia during the First World War, and are pictured here at Ahmadnagar, India, where they were sent to guard German prisoners of war.

Soldiers of the 4th Battalion, Dorset Regiment, at Ahmadnagar, 1915.

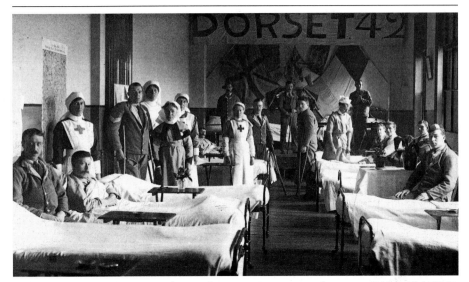

Members of the Voluntary Aid Detachment (VAD) in Dorchester, *c.* 1916. This VAD Auxiliary Hospital was located in the Church Street Hall, and Mrs Ackland of Wolleston House was the commandant. Although members of the VAD worked entirely voluntarily, they were much involved in the hard reality of wartime nursing, and by the end of the war had proved their usefulness. They were much loved by the convalescing soldiers, who nicknamed these angels with red crosses on their uniforms 'Very Artful Darlings' or 'Victim Always Dies'.

Dorchester Boys' School Army Cadets, Colliton Street, *c.* 1916.

Members of the Dorchester United Church of England Temperance Societies in the soldiers' tea and rest room, Corn Exchange, *c.* 1917. Left to right: Miss Whittle, Mrs Pickett, Canon Coote, Mrs Coote, Mrs Logan, Miss Holbeck, Miss Cross.

During the First World War, the Church of England Temperance Societies made arrangements to keep the temptation of alchohol away from the soldiers, and to make life more pleasant and agreeable for them. A committee of ladies were in charge of a well-stocked tea and rest room, and here we can see the lady helpers, including Mrs Davage, Mrs Batchelor and Miss Pearce, ready to serve the men.

The internment camp, Poundbury. During the First World War, several thousand German prisoners of war were held here. During their enforced stay forty-eight prisoners died; they are commemorated with a memorial in Fordington cemetery.

The German prisoner of war camp at Poundbury, c. 1916.

Dorset VAD, 20 July 1923. This photograph was taken at the time of the visit of the Prince of Wales to Dorchester. Mrs Marsden is in the centre in black, with Miss Marsden and Miss Hoar on her left. Mrs Vidler is sitting cross-legged in front of Mrs Marsden.

A group of volunteer air-raid wardens standing outside their sandbagged post, named Windy Corner Post, 1942. Note the tape on the windows to stop glass splintering in the event of a bomb blast.

Leaders in Dorchester Civil Defence during the Second World War, 1942. Left to right: D. Jackman (ARP Controller), Dr A.P. Platt (Scientific Advisers Division, Ministry of Food), J.H. Dean (Food Decontamination Officer), C. Williams (Civil Experimental Officer), H. Jewell (Deputy Divisional Gas Liaison Officer, Ministry of Food).

Land Girls marching in High West Street, c. 1943. Many girls chose to work on the land for their war service, and they quickly settled down to all the general work on the farm. For many of them, who came from towns, this was quite an experience, but they soon proved their worth, fulfilling a vital job during the Second World War.

Members of the Dorchester Royal Observer Corps at their post in the town, *c.* 1943. Left to right, Messrs Tomlinson, Wells, Roger and Houghton. The Observers rendered valuable service during the Second World War. There were posts throughout the country, where watches were kept night and day for any sight or sound of enemy aircraft. Britain's defences would be set in motion if these devoted watchers in their far-flung outposts spotted anything untoward.

The Dorchester Royal Observer Corps, *c.* 1943. Left to right: -?-, Joe Wynn and 'Sailor' Rogers.

The Dorchester Regiment in Maumbury Rings during the Second World War.

Members of the American Anti-Aircraft Unit at Poundbury, May 1944. They were Section 4, 1st Platoon, B Battery of the 204th Anti-Aircraft Artillery Automatic Weapons Battalion of the 49th AAA Brigade, attached to the 1st Army and the 9th Airforce. Back row, left to right: Moses, Pate, Gordon, Brooks. Second row: Renfroe, Cohen, Partin, Cakenhead, Channel, Davis. Front row: Weeks, De Pietro, Morris, Philips.

Mrs N. Parsons and the US Transport Officers for embarkation of the US army to France, 1944.

Dorchester Civil Defence, 1945. Included in the group are Maj. W. Fletcher, Dr T. Stallybrass, Mr F. Day, Mr E. Moran, Mr J. Steptoe, Col. S.W. Sackville, Mr F.L. Maskell, Mr D. Cogswell, Mr J. Chesterfield, Lt.-Col. F.B. Nixon and Lord Shaftesbury.

Dorchester Civil Defence stand down, 1945. Back row, left to right: Watson, Harvey, Cogswell. Second row: Day, Steptoe, Freeman, -?-, Mortimer, Lane, Leave, Warren. Front row: Maskell (standing), Moran, Hamilton, Nixon, Brutton, Smallman, Swain, Jackman, Chesterfield (standing).

SECTION SIX

Sport

Dorchester Grammar School Football Team, First XI, 1907/8. Back row, left to right: Michell, Hopkinson, Mr Collier, Hawkes, Jackman. Front row: Browne, Dawes, Budden, MacSwiney (Capt.), Hunt, Wrisbery, Jackman.

Dorchester Hockey Club, *c.* 1900. The club played on the recreation ground by the railway embankment. Back row, left to right: J. Drake, -?-, A.R. Edwards, S. Club, ? Subell, -?-, J. Dean. Second row, seated: -?-, W.J. Simmons, -?-, ? Dobell. Front row, on ground: A. Hill, W. Dundew.

A fine group of cricketers, taken at The Barracks, *c.* 1895. The British officer in plain clothes was scrutinized almost as carefully as when he was wearing uniform. Note the variety of head-gear worn by the men – assorted but acceptable.

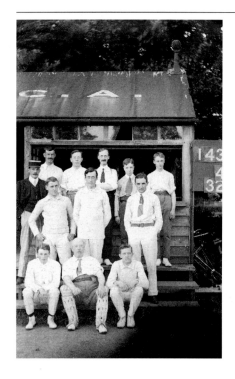

YMCA cricket team, *c.* 1910. Those present include Douglas Carey Reading, Gilbert Laws and Mr Rankin.

The start of the Dorchester versus Weymouth Harriers race, *c.* 1900. The man in the front is obviously taking great pride in his new bicycle.

Dorchester YMCA Harriers, 1907. The faces of the team members show a confident pride in their past achievements, and a determination for future ones.

Members of the Dorchester YMCA team and the Weymouth YMCA team at the start of the Harriers race, *c.* 1910. The event was won by Dorchester.

Dorchester YMCA Harriers, 1911.

Dorchester Mayor Joe Porter starting the YMCA Harriers Handicap race, 1912. The two competitors were Mr Angell and Mr Savage.

Dorset County Rifle Club, Poundbury, *c.* 1951. Members present include Capt W.V. Richardson and Mr O.C. Vidler.

C.M. Cave, Capt W.V. Richardson and, pictured on the left, O.C. Vidler from Dorchester, at Bisley *c.* 1950.

SECTION SEVEN

Transport

Godwin's delivery cart *c.* 1890. Godwin's were in business at this date at 10 High West Street, and this smart turn-out was obviously for a publicity photograph.

Driving the car is Tom Stone, the first mechanic for Tilley's, the motor engineers,
c. 1904.

Channon & Sons, High East Street, 1905. Ernest Channon, bottom right, stands by the Channon car which he designed and produced.

Dorchester men at the start of a day's outing in a motor bus. One of the changes after the First World War was the arrival of these vehicles into all parts of Dorset.

A Ford fourteen-seater carrier's van belonging to Bales, one of the railway carriers in Dorchester, *c.* 1925. The van left the Phoenix at 16 High Street on Wednesdays and Saturdays, plying between Waddock and Dorchester. The seats inside were all removable, and on the day this photograph was taken it was being loaded up with furniture.

Dorchester Carnival, *c.* 1936. During the annual carnival, local lorries were always in demand for tableaux.

The steam plough works of the Eddison Rolling Co. Ltd, *c.* 1886. This photograph of Eddison's yard presents a sight that will rarely be seen again, as the romance of steam has been all but completely replaced by the more efficient internal combustion engine.

This engine is possibly No. 40, *Windsor*, of the South Western Railway, photographed at Dorchester in 1859. Designed by Joseph Beattie and built at Nine Elms in 1852, the *Windsor* had 5 ft 6 in driving wheels and rear coupled inside cylinders.

Telephone No. 134   Postal and Telegraphic Address: "MARVIN LOCK, DORCHESTER"

OLDEST ESTABLISHED

J. MARVIN LOCK

House, Steam & Gas Coal & Coke Contractor

DORCHESTER

Wharfs at: Gt. Western & Southern Railway Stations

OFFICES:

1 NORTH SQUARE & GREAT WESTERN STATION

Connected by Telephone

Agent for : SUTTON & CO., GENERAL CARRIERS
the WEST OF ENGLAND SACK CONTRACTORS, LTD.
and WESTLAKE'S SACKS, LTD.

COAL Delivered to the Country Districts
by Steam Wagon and Petrol Lorries at
SPECIAL PRICES

*Quotations for any description of Coal Delivered Free to any Railway Station by the
TRUCK LOAD AT COLLIERY PRICES.*

ROCK SALT and AGRICULTURAL   — Also a Large Assortment of—
SALT KEPT IN STOCK.   BEST YORKSHIRE GRINDING STONE

PUBLIC WEIGHBRIDGES AT BOTH STATIONS

Advertisement for J. Marvin Lock, *c.* 1926.

The Ramblers Cycling Club, Easter Monday, 1900. The cyclists are about to leave on a trip to Lulworth.

Acknowledgements

I am grateful to all those who have helped in the compilation of this book by contributing valuable information. Thanks must go to Lyn Marshall, without whose help I could not have produced the book. Edna Everitt gave much appreciated assistance, and I am grateful to my wife, Carol, for her encouragement and help. Thanks also to Alan Sutton Publishing Ltd for their assistance. The photographs in this book all come from the wonderful collection in the photographic record department of the Dorset County Museum. I am indebted to Richard de Peyer, the Curator, for allowing these pictures to be used, and for the kindness and help shown to me by his staff, making the task of putting together this book a pleasure.

BRITAIN IN OLD PHOTOGRAPHS

To order any of these titles please telephone 0453 731114

ALDERNEY

Alderney: A Second Selection, *B Bonnard*

BEDFORDSHIRE

Bedfordshire at Work, *N Lutt*

BERKSHIRE

Maidenhead, *M Hayles & D Hedges*
Around Maidenhead, *M Hayles & B Hedges*
Reading, *P Southerton*
Reading: A Second Selection, *P Southerton*
Sandhurst and Crowthorne, *K Dancy*
Around Slough, *J Hunter & K Hunter*
Around Thatcham, *P Allen*
Around Windsor, *B Hedges*

BUCKINGHAMSHIRE

Buckingham and District, *R Cook*
High Wycombe, *R Goodearl*
Around Stony Stratford, *A Lambert*

CHESHIRE

Cheshire Railways, *M Hitches*
Chester, *S Nichols*

CLWYD

Clwyd Railways, *M Hitches*

CLYDESDALE

Clydesdale, *Lesmahagow Parish Historical Association*

CORNWALL

Cornish Coast, *T Bowden*
Falmouth, *P Gilson*
Lower Fal, *P Gilson*
Around Padstow, *M McCarthy*
Around Penzance, *J Holmes*
Penzance and Newlyn, *J Holmes*
Around Truro, *A Lyne*
Upper Fal, *P Gilson*

CUMBERLAND

Cockermouth and District, *J Bernard Bradbury*
Keswick and the Central Lakes, *J Marsh*
Around Penrith, *F Boyd*
Around Whitehaven, *H Fancy*

DERBYSHIRE

Derby, *D Buxton*
Around Matlock, *D Barton*

DEVON

Colyton and Seaton, *T Gosling*
Dawlish and Teignmouth, *G Gosling*
Devon Aerodromes, *K Saunders*
Exeter, *P Thomas*
Exmouth and Budleigh Salterton, *T Gosling*
From Haldon to Mid-Dartmoor, *T Hall*
Honiton and the Otter Valley, *J Yallop*
Around Kingsbridge, *K Tanner*
Around Seaton and Sidmouth, *T Gosling*
Seaton, Axminster and Lyme Regis, *T Gosling*

DORSET

Around Blandford Forum, *B Cox*
Bournemouth, *M Colman*
Bridport and the Bride Valley, *J Burrell & S Humphries*
Dorchester, *T Gosling*
Around Gillingham, *P Crocker*

DURHAM

Darlington, *G Flynn*
Darlington: A Second Selection, *G Flynn*
Durham People, *M Richardson*
Houghton-le-Spring and Hetton-le-Hole, *K Richardson*
Houghton-le-Spring and Hetton-le-Hole:
    A Second Selection, *K Richardson*
Sunderland, *S Miller & B Bell*
Teesdale, *D Coggins*
Teesdale: A Second Selection, *P Raine*
Weardale, *J Crosby*
Weardale: A Second Selection, *J Crosby*

DYFED

Aberystwyth and North Ceredigion,
    Dyfed Cultural Services Dept
Haverfordwest, *Dyfed Cultural Services Dept*
Upper Tywi Valley, *Dyfed Cultural Services Dept*

ESSEX

Around Grays, *B Evans*

GLOUCESTERSHIRE

Along the Avon from Stratford to Tewkesbury, *J Jeremiah*
Cheltenham: A Second Selection, *R Whiting*
Cheltenham at War, *P Gill*
Cirencester, *J Welsford*
Around Cirencester, *E Cuss & P Griffiths*
Forest, The, *D Mullin*
Gloucester, *J Voyce*
Around Gloucester, *A Sutton*
Gloucester: From the Walwin Collection, *J Voyce*
North Cotswolds, *D Viner*
Severn Vale, *A Sutton*
Stonehouse to Painswick, *A Sutton*
Stroud and the Five Valleys, *S Gardiner & L Padin*
Stroud and the Five Valleys: A Second Selection,
    S Gardiner & L Padin
Stroud's Golden Valley, *S Gardiner & L Padin*
Stroudwater and Thames & Severn Canals,
    E Cuss & S Gardiner
Stroudwater and Thames & Severn Canals: A Second
    Selection, *E Cuss & S Gardiner*
Tewkesbury and the Vale of Gloucester, *C Hilton*
Thornbury to Berkeley, *J Hudson*
Uley, Dursley and Cam, *A Sutton*
Wotton-under-Edge to Chipping Sodbury, *A Sutton*

GWYNEDD

Anglesey, *M Hitches*
Gwynedd Railways, *M Hitches*
Around Llandudno, *M Hitches*
Vale of Conwy, *M Hitches*

HAMPSHIRE

Gosport, *J Sadden*
Portsmouth, *P Rogers & D Francis*

HEREFORDSHIRE

Herefordshire, *A Sandford*

HERTFORDSHIRE

Barnet, *I Norrie*
Hitchin, *A Fleck*
St Albans, *S Mullins*
Stevenage, *M Appleton*

ISLE OF MAN

The Tourist Trophy, *B Snelling*

ISLE OF WIGHT

Newport, *D Parr*
Around Ryde, *D Parr*

JERSEY

Jersey: A Third Selection, *R Lemprière*

KENT

Bexley, *M Scott*
Broadstairs and St Peter's, *J Whyman*
Bromley, Keston and Hayes, *M Scott*
Canterbury: A Second Selection, *D Butler*
Chatham and Gillingham, *P MacDougall*
Chatham Dockyard, *P MacDougall*
Deal, *J Broady*
Early Broadstairs and St Peter's, *B Wootton*
East Kent at War, *D Collyer*
Eltham, *J Kennett*
Folkestone: A Second Selection, *A Taylor & E Rooney*
Goudhurst to Tenterden, *A Guilmant*
Gravesend, *R Hiscock*
Around Gravesham, *R Hiscock & D Grierson*
Herne Bay, *J Hawkins*
Lympne Airport, *D Collyer*
Maidstone, *I Hales*
Margate, *R Clements*
RAF Hawkinge, *R Humphreys*
RAF Manston, *RAF Manston History Club*
RAF Manston: A Second Selection,
    RAF Manston History Club
Ramsgate and Thanet Life, *D Perkins*
Romney Marsh, *E Carpenter*
Sandwich, *C Wanostrocht*
Around Tonbridge, *C Bell*
Tunbridge Wells, *M Rowlands & I Beavis*
Tunbridge Wells: A Second Selection,
    M Rowlands & I Beavis
Around Whitstable, *C Court*
Wingham, Adisham and Littlebourne, *M Crane*

LANCASHIRE

Around Barrow-in-Furness, *J Garbutt & J Marsh*
Blackpool, *C Rothwell*
Bury, *J Hudson*
Chorley and District, *J Smith*
Fleetwood, *C Rothwell*
Heywood, *J Hudson*
Around Kirkham, *C Rothwell*
Lancashire North of the Sands, *J Garbutt & J Marsh*
Around Lancaster, *S Ashworth*
Lytham St Anne's, *C Rothwell*
North Fylde, *C Rothwell*
Radcliffe, *J Hudson*
Rossendale, *B Moore & N Dunnachie*

LEICESTERSHIRE

Around Ashby-de-la-Zouch, *K Hillier*
Charnwood Forest, *I Keil, W Humphrey & D Wix*
Leicester, *D Burton*
Leicester: A Second Selection, *D Burton*
Melton Mowbray, *T Hickman*
Around Melton Mowbray, *T Hickman*
River Soar, *D Wix, P Shacklock & I Keil*
Rutland, *T Clough*
Vale of Belvoir, *T Hickman*
Around the Welland Valley, *S Mastoris*

LINCOLNSHIRE

Grimsby, *J Tierney*
Around Grimsby, *J Tierney*
Grimsby Docks, *J Tierney*
Lincoln, *D Cuppleditch*

Scunthorpe, *D Taylor*
Skegness, *W Kime*
Around Skegness, *W Kime*

LONDON

Balham and Tooting, *P Loobey*
Crystal Palace, Penge & Anerley, *M Scott*
Greenwich and Woolwich, *K Clark*
Hackney: A Second Selection, *D Mander*
Lewisham and Deptford, *J Coulter*
Lewisham and Deptford: A Second Selection, *J Coulter*
Streatham, *P Loobey*
Around Whetstone and North Finchley, *J Heathfield*
Woolwich, *B Evans*

MONMOUTHSHIRE

Chepstow and the River Wye, *A Rainsbury*
Monmouth and the River Wye, *Monmouth Museum*

NORFOLK

Great Yarmouth, *M Teun*
Norwich, *M Colman*
Wymondham and Attleborough, *P Yaxley*

NORTHAMPTONSHIRE

Around Stony Stratford, *A Lambert*

NOTTINGHAMSHIRE

Arnold and Bestwood, *M Spick*
Arnold and Bestwood: A Second Selection, *M Spick*
Changing Face of Nottingham, *G Oldfield*
Mansfield, *Old Mansfield Society*
Around Newark, *T Warner*
Nottingham: 1944–1974, *D Whitworth*
Sherwood Forest, *D Ottewell*
Victorian Nottingham, *M Payne*

OXFORDSHIRE

Around Abingdon, *P Horn*
Banburyshire, *M Barnett & S Gosling*
Burford, *A Jewell*
Around Didcot and the Hagbournes, *B Lingham*
Garsington, *M Gunther*
Around Henley-on-Thames, *S Ellis*
Oxford: The University, *J Rhodes*
Thame to Watlington, *N Hood*
Around Wallingford, *D Beasley*
Witney, *T Worley*
Around Witney, *C Mitchell*
Witney District, *T Worley*
Around Woodstock, *J Bond*

POWYS

Brecon, *Brecknock Museum*
Welshpool, *E Bredsdorff*

SHROPSHIRE

Shrewsbury, *D Trumper*
Whitchurch to Market Drayton, *M Morris*

SOMERSET

Bath, *J Hudson*
Bridgwater and the River Parrett, *R Fitzhugh*
Bristol, *D Moorcroft & N Campbell-Sharp*
Changing Face of Keynsham,
  B Lowe & M Whitehead

Chard and Ilminster, *G Gosling & F Huddy*
Crewkerne and the Ham Stone Villages,
  G Gosling & F Huddy
Around Keynsham and Saltford, *B Lowe & T Brown*
Midsomer Norton and Radstock, *C Howell*
Somerton, Ilchester and Langport, *G Gosling & F Huddy*
Taunton, *N Chipchase*
Around Taunton, *N Chipchase*
Wells, *C Howell*
Weston-Super-Mare, *S Poole*
Around Weston-Super-Mare, *S Poole*
West Somerset Villages, *K Houghton & L Thomas*

STAFFORDSHIRE

Aldridge, *J Farrow*
Bilston, *E Rees*
Black Country Transport: Aviation, *A Brew*
Around Burton upon Trent, *G Sowerby & R Farman*
Bushbury, *A Chatwin, M Mills & E Rees*
Around Cannock, *M Mills & S Belcher*
Around Leek, *R Poole*
Lichfield, *H Clayton & K Simmons*
Around Pattingham and Wombourne, *M Griffiths,*
  P Leigh & M Mills
Around Rugeley, *T Randall & J Anslow*
Smethwick, *J Maddison*
Stafford, *J Anslow & T Randall*
Around Stafford, *J Anslow & T Randall*
Stoke-on-Trent, *I Lawley*
Around Tamworth, *R Sulima*
Around Tettenhall and Codsall, *M Mills*
Tipton, Wednesbury and Darlaston, *R Pearson*
Walsall, *D Gilbert & M Lewis*
Wednesbury, *I Bott*
West Bromwich, *R Pearson*

SUFFOLK

Ipswich: A Second Selection, *D Kindred*
Around Ipswich, *D Kindred*
Around Mildenhall, *C Dring*
Southwold to Aldeburgh, *H Phelps*
Around Woodbridge, *H Phelps*

SURREY

Cheam and Belmont, *P Berry*
Croydon, *S Bligh*
Dorking and District, *K Harding*
Around Dorking, *A Jackson*
Around Epsom, *P Berry*
Farnham: A Second Selection, *J Parratt*
Around Haslemere and Hindhead, *T Winter & G Collyer*
Richmond, *Richmond Local History Society*
Sutton, *P Berry*

SUSSEX

Arundel and the Arun Valley, *J Godfrey*
Bishopstone and Seaford, *P Pople & P Berry*
Brighton and Hove, *J Middleton*
Brighton and Hove: A Second Selection, *J Middleton*
Around Crawley, *M Goldsmith*
Hastings, *P Haines*
Hastings: A Second Selection, *P Haines*
Around Haywards Heath, *J Middleton*
Around Heathfield, *A Gillet & B Russell*
Around Heathfield: A Second Selection,
  A Gillet & B Russell
High Weald, *B Harwood*
High Weald: A Second Selection, *B Harwood*
Horsham and District, *T Wales*

Lewes, *J Middleton*
RAF Tangmere, *A Saunders*
Around Rye, *A Dickinson*
Around Worthing, *S White*

WARWICKSHIRE

Along the Avon from Stratford to Tewkesbury, *J Jeremiah*
Bedworth, *J Burton*
Coventry, *D McGrory*
Around Coventry, *D McGrory*
Nuneaton, *S Clews & S Vaughan*
Around Royal Leamington Spa, *J Cameron*
Around Royal Leamington Spa: A Second Selection,
  J Cameron
Around Warwick, *R Booth*

WESTMORLAND

Eden Valley, *J Marsh*
Kendal, *M & P Duff*
South Westmorland Villages, *J Marsh*
Westmorland Lakes, *J Marsh*

WILTSHIRE

Around Amesbury, *P Daniels*
Chippenham and Lacock, *A Wilson & M Wilson*
Around Corsham and Box, *A Wilson & M Wilson*
Around Devizes, *D Buxton*
Around Highworth, *G Tanner*
Around Highworth and Faringdon, *G Tanner*
Around Malmesbury, *A Wilson*
Marlborough: A Second Selection, *P Colman*
Around Melksham,
  Melksham and District Historical Association
Nadder Valley, *R. Sawyer*
Salisbury, *P Saunders*
Salisbury: A Second Selection, *P Daniels*
Salisbury: A Third Selection, *P Daniels*
Around Salisbury, *P Daniels*
Swindon: A Third Selection, *The Swindon Society*
Swindon: A Fourth Selection, *The Swindon Society*
Trowbridge, *M Marshman*
Around Wilton, *P Daniels*
Around Wootton Bassett, Cricklade and Purton, *T Sharp*

WORCESTERSHIRE

Evesham to Bredon, *F Archer*
Around Malvern, *K Smith*
Around Pershore, *M Dowty*
Redditch and the Needle District, *R Saunders*
Redditch: A Second Selection, *R Saunders*
Around Tenbury Wells, *D Green*
Worcester, *M Dowty*
Around Worcester, *R Jones*
Worcester in a Day, *M Dowty*
Worcestershire at Work, *R Jones*

YORKSHIRE

Huddersfield: A Second Selection, *H Wheeler*
Huddersfield: A Third Selection, *H Wheeler*
Leeds Road and Rail, *R Vickers*
Pontefract, *R van Riel*
Scarborough, *D Coggins*
Scarborough's War Years, *R Percy*
Skipton and the Dales, *Friends of the Craven Museum*
Around Skipton-in-Craven, *Friends of the Craven Museum*
Yorkshire Wolds, *I & M Sumner*